JOAN OF ARC

FRENCH SOLDIER AND SAINT

JOAN OF ARC
FRENCH SOLDIER AND SAINT

PHILIP WOLNY

Britannica®
Educational Publishing

IN ASSOCIATION WITH

ROSEN
EDUCATIONAL SERVICES

Published in 2018 by Britannica Educational Publishing (a trademark of Encyclopædia Britannica, Inc.) in association with The Rosen Publishing Group, Inc.
29 East 21st Street, New York, NY 10010

Distributed exclusively by Rosen Publishing.
To see additional Britannica Educational Publishing titles, go to rosenpublishing.com.

First Edition

Britannica Educational Publishing
J.E. Luebering: Executive Director, Core Editorial
Andrea R. Field: Managing Editor, Compton's by Britannica

Rosen Publishing
Heather Moore Niver: Editor
Nelson Sá: Art Director
Michael Moy: Designer
Cindy Reiman: Photography Manager
Heather Moore Niver: Photo Researcher

Library of Congress Cataloging-in-Publication Data

Names: Wolny, Philip, author.
Title: Joan of Arc : French soldier and saint / Philip Wolny.
Description: New York : Britannica Educational Publishing in association with Rosen Educational Services, [2018] | Series: Women who changed history | Includes bibliographical references and index. | Audience: Grades 5-8.
Identifiers: LCCN 2016057946| ISBN 9781680486476 (library bound : alk. paper) | ISBN 9781680486452 (pbk. : alk. paper) | ISBN 9781680486469 (6-pack : alk. paper)
Subjects: LCSH: Joan, of Arc, Saint, 1412-1431—Juvenile literature. | Christian women saints—France—Biography—Juvenile literature. | France—History—Charles VII, 1422-1461—Juvenile literature.
Classification: LCC DC103.5 .W65 2018 | DDC 944.026092 [B] —dc23
LC record available at https://lccn.loc.gov/2016057946

CONTENTS

INTRODUCTION

More than six hundred years ago, in the early fifteenth century, the nation of France was at war with England. They had been in conflict off and on for decades, since 1337, over who would control much of the territory of France itself. This set of conflicts was known as the Hundred Years' War, and it occurred toward the end of what we now call the Middle Ages, the period of European history that included the era of knights and chivalry.

By the early 1400s, France's luck against the English seemed to have faded. While France was, for the most part, richer, larger, and more populous, the English often had the upper hand. Their better weapons, including their longbows, allowed them to frequently beat back much larger French forces, including the knights mounted on horseback, called cavalry.

The newest stage in the war, called the Lancastrian War, began in 1415 with the English invasion of the northwest coastal area of France known as Normandy. England soon gained control of about one-third of French territory—all of France north of the Loire River, including Paris. It was a time in which the French struggled for hope.

Even as the English seemed unstoppable, hope was bound to return, even if the French did not know it yet. Around 1412 a baby named Joan had been born in a small village called Domrémy in the eastern countryside. Her parents, Jacques d'Arc and Isabelle Romée, were landowners and farmers, and respected members of their village.

This 1854 painting by Jean-Auguste-Dominique Ingres, entitled *Joan of Arc at the Coronation of Charles VII in Reims Cathedral*, depicts the heroine at the moment of one of her greatest triumphs.

Under normal circumstances, Joan would probably have grown up to live a quiet, regular life. She and her four siblings were well off enough, and perhaps Joan would have been married to another middle-class farmer in the area. Most women—and even men, for that matter, unless they were bound for jobs in the clerical or legal fields, or for university studies—did not learn to read or write. Joan lived pretty much the same life and did the same things as her siblings and peers of her age.

Most women who were famous or influential then were royalty, or otherwise married into power or influence. But an entirely different life and destiny lined up for the young woman who would become known as the Maid of Orléans. Rather than remain in her small village, she would defy the typical roles a girl and woman usually took during this era. Joan of Arc would instead become one of the most romantic figures in European history. She would become a leader, a warrior, and a French national hero. To the enemies of her people, the English, she would be a thorn in their side, and a heretic. But she would also be a reputed prophet and holy messenger who would become famous for her heroism, devotion, and ultimate sacrifice for her faith and nation. Eventually she would even become a saint.

CHAPTER ONE

THE VISIONS OF A YOUNG WOMAN

The tiny village of Domrémy rarely figured into important events. Less than two hundred people lived there, mostly growing crops or making wine. Most French people were faithful Roman Catholics, and Domrémy's villagers were no different. As historian Donald Spoto writes in *Joan: The Mysterious Life of the Heretic Who Became a Saint*, "faith and its practice were mainstream aspects of medieval life," and the "language of faith was like a common country in which all people lived."

A RESPONSIBLE CHILD

Joan of Arc (in French Jeanne d'Arc) was probably born in 1412, although some accounts

This image shows a room in the house where Joan is believed to have been born, in modern-day Domrémy-la-Pucelle, France.

Joan's simple and unremarkable origin as a farm girl who tended sheep is shown in this sixteenth-century illustration.

say it may have been a year earlier. At the time, few people cared very much about their exact date of birth or age, and these were mostly not recorded in any official way. Joan learned to spin, sew, and cook, and also to love God. Though most young people prayed, Joan was known for being particularly devout, and prayed in church much of the time.

BORN INTO WARTIME

Despite its name, the Hundred Years' War actually lasted about 116 years, and was not continuous. It was a series of conflicts making up one of recorded history's longest wars. The combatants, or participants, were England and its supporters, including the French duchy of Burgundy, versus the kingdom of France and its allies.

When France's monarch died in 1328, England's King Edward III, who also controlled parts of southwestern France under the title of duke, sought to become the French king, too. This prompted a prolonged struggle over French lands that was broken up by periods of truce. France even had the upper hand for a time.

But a period of civil war among the French themselves around 1407 weakened them, and also inspired England's Henry V to invade Normandy in 1415. He and his allies, the Burgundians, soon controlled the major southwest region of Aquitaine, and all of France north of the Loire River, including the capital, Paris. They also ruled Reims, the city where French kings were traditionally crowned. This prevented the newly established heir to the French throne, Charles VII, from being crowned the true king. But a new era and new champion would soon arise to break this stalemate.

Joan was a responsible young woman who helped her family with farming and livestock. She attended church often. This is where she learned her Bible lessons and stories, and examined church art and artifacts, such as paintings. During mass, she learned about the important saints. For Catholics, saints are heroic defenders of the faith.

DIVINE MESSAGES

Joan was only about thirteen when she first saw a heavenly vision, around 1424 or 1425, while in her father's garden on a summer day. A bright light surrounded her. A voice told her to be a good girl, obey her mother, and to faithfully attend church. Initially she was scared, but soon was comforted. She later claimed that St. Michael, considered one of the most powerful archangels (high-ranking angels in God's service), was her first "visitor."

SAINTLY VOICES

Other visitations followed, including from St. Margaret of Antioch and St. Catherine of Alexandria. St. Catherine was a symbol of Christian heroism, and the patron of young women and girls, while St. Margaret was particularly beloved in Joan's region, and was the patroness of people who were falsely accused of crimes or wrongdoing. Joan believed sincerely that these voices spoke for God.

II

Dès l'âge de treize ans
elle entendit des voix qui lui
ordonnèrent avec insistance
d'aller sauver la France, alors
envahie par les Anglais.

SAZERAC
Phot.

CJA

CROISSANT
PARIS

3840

There are many images like this one, which depicts the visions and voices that Joan claimed inspired her to take up her struggle against the English and their French collaborators.

Rather than being an isolated incident, Joan's visions of angelic visitations continued throughout her adolescence and convinced her to take action.

According to Spoto, "Over the next three years, she was summoned by the voices 'to come to the aid of the king of France.'" The French "king," Charles VII, was technically not crowned yet, because the coronation site of the city of Reims was still in enemy hands. Thus, he was known as the Dauphin, French for "heir apparent."

JOAN GAINS RESOLVE

Joan kept these divine experiences secret at first, and never actually specified how often and when many of them occurred. She only revealed them to two friends. Partly it was because she feared disbelief by her parents and parish priest. She also was confused about what to actually do about them. In addition, those who claimed to have visions were sometimes considered mentally unwell, or even painted as heretics (dangerous unbelievers) or witches. Witches could be harshly punished, including being tortured or put to death.

Later on, she related how she prayed for guidance and to give herself time to think deeply on them. She was still just a young girl, after all. It was nearly four years from the start of her visitations until she took concrete action. Her visions had by then become so real to her that she decided she had to take action.

CHAPTER TWO

MEETING DESTINY

It was in 1428 when the voices told Joan she had to act. They inspired her to make her way to the nearby town of Vaucoulers. This was 10 miles (16 kilometers) north of Domrémy, so Joan had to figure out a reason or pretense for going there. She hoped to plead her case to Robert de Baudricort, the captain of the town's French military garrison, part of the army loyal to the Dauphin. And she hoped the captain would escort her to the Dauphin's headquarters at Chinon, about 260 miles (420 kilometers) away.

Her mother's cousin was in her last months of pregnancy near Vaucoulers, and Joan volunteered to go help around their house. She then convinced a relative to take her to the garrison. Unfortunately, Joan was not taken seriously, and was turned away. She returned home, and her parents were clueless about her visit's true purpose.

When Joan reached the age of sixteen, her parents tried to arrange a marriage for her with a boy, a common arrangement then. But Joan stood firm and refused to be married. She even won in local court when the family of the boy protested that Joan and her family had broken their

Shown here are ruins of the Great Hall of the Château of Chinon, where the Dauphin had his court and where Joan first met him in 1429. A project to restore the royal château was completed in 2010.

arrangement. This was the only time she actively defied her parents. Secretly, her major motivation was to keep a vow of chastity to herself and God, until her purpose was met and her mission accomplished, whatever it might be.

The enemy fueled Joan's resolve in July 1428, when the Burgundians pillaged Domrémy and neighboring villages. Joan's family and many of her neighbors escaped ahead of time to another town. Upon returning, they were saddened to find much of their village damaged or destroyed. News arrived that October that Orléans, the last major city still loyal to the French, had been besieged by English forces.

A CRUCIAL DECISION

Along with her faith, another quality of Joan's that others respected was her persistence. She secretly left home and visited Vaucoulers again in January 1429 to again try to convince the Dauphin's soldiers to take her to see him. This time, she remained patient, and after some time in town, spending every day at church, she prevailed. She impressed many of them with her faith and integrity, and persuaded the captain to take her to Chinon, where she would tell the Dauphin about her visions and offer her service.

Joan, dressed in men's clothes, left for the trip about February 13, accompanied by six men-at-arms. Her attire served a couple of purposes. It was for comfort, but it also

Joan prays at the foot of a statue of the Virgin Mary. Images of the Maid as a devout and incorruptible soldier of her faith are part of her legend.

VISIONARY OR NOT?

Historians and laymen alike fascinated with Joan have long wondered whether she truly received divine guidance. Although a small minority believes she may have lied, most experts do not doubt her sincerity. Others have theorized that there were other explanations.

Among these are theories that Joan may have suffered from psychological issues or health problems. Some feel that perhaps disorders like schizophrenia or epilepsy caused her to imagine the visions. Other theories argue that Joan had an untreated ear infection, brain lesion, or even intense migraines, which caused her to hallucinate. Another curious theory was that she had caught bovine tuberculosis from her family's cows, which has been known to cause dementia and seizures.

Still, by all accounts, in every other way, Joan was smart, logical, well spoken, polite, and thoughtful. Physically, she was able to keep up with many of the military men of her day, and had a mind for strategy. It is highly unlikely that she could have kept symptoms of mental illness hidden from others so successfully. Whether one fully believes in Joan of Arc being a divine messenger, it is hard to deny that she was inspired to heroism and great things.

helped conceal the fact that she was a woman from potential enemies, including bandits. With her hair cut short, Joan resembled a young page—in other words, a young knight's apprentice and helper.

A medieval tapestry depicts Joan, dressed in full armor, arriving in Chinon, where she is greeted by Charles VII.

AT THE COURT OF CHARLES VII

The group traveled through the enemy-held heart of France for eleven days before they reached the Dauphin. Just outside Chinon, Joan dictated a letter to her parents revealing her whereabouts and mission. Her parents soon sent her brothers, Pierre and Jean, to help protect her.

The Dauphin's counselors met her first. Two of them questioned her extensively. One felt she was worthy of an audience with Charles, while the other believed her insane.

An illustration portrays the moment when Joan, according to legend, picked out the Dauphin correctly from among the other members of his court.

Captain de Baudricort wrote to give his endorsement, too. Finally, she was invited to see Charles on March 6.

As a test, the Dauphin hid himself among his courtiers. Joan, however, went directly to Charles and greeted him. Perhaps she saw through the trick, or was directed by some kind of second sight. Nevertheless, it was the words she uttered next that captured the Dauphin's imagination, according to Donald Spoto: "My most eminent Lord Dauphin, I have come, sent by God, to bring help to you and to the kingdom."

CHAPTER THREE

GOING TO WAR

Months of doubt and indecision followed while Joan was questioned by the Dauphin and his court. While someone speaking like Joan did might nowadays inspire some doubt, the people of the medieval era did not dismiss such statements as easily. Her seriousness and sincerity were very convincing.

In addition, Joan went to the town of Poitiers for three weeks of questioning by church authorities who were allied to the Dauphin's cause. While no transcripts of these examinations have survived, it is known that Joan told the churchmen that it was not at Poitiers that she would give proof of her mission, but rather at Orléans, which had been under English siege for months.

The French royalists held few major territories, they had nearly run out of money to even fight the war, and the siege of Orléans had made things seem grimmer than ever. Could the appearance of this unusual and intense young woman be a sign their fortunes would change? The church authorities ultimately recommended that the desperate situation at Orléans made it necessary for the Dauphin to try whatever he could.

The secretary of the Parliament of Paris, Clément de Fauquembergue, made this sketch of Joan in 1429. It is believed to be one of the earliest images of her.

PREPARATIONS

Joan's arrival seemed to inspire a change in the Dauphin. He had previously seemed indecisive, afraid, and to almost have lost the will to fight on. When she returned from Poitiers, Joan was quickly given lodging in the castle at Chinon, and was assigned a page of her own, such as a knight or other royal court member often had.

Joan was more humble than she was patient, however. She firmly believed that the siege of Orléans should be lifted as soon as possible. The ultimate goal was to beat back the English and Burgundians, and clear the way to Reims for the king's coronation. Joan dictated defiant letters to the English.

Soon after, an army was gathered at Tours. Joan would accompany them, and eventually take charge. The Dauphin equipped Joan with armor, attendants, and horses. Her brothers arrived, and would seldom be far from her side. She had her standard and banner decorated with the images and name of Jesus Christ. She declared that a sword for her to use would be found in the church of Sainte-Catherine-de-Fierbois, and one was in fact discovered there.

ONWARD TO ORLÉANS

In late April, it was time to strike. Miraculously, it was Joan who would rise to the occasion and lead the campaign. Orléans was ringed by English strongholds. Joan entered

A 1903 engraving featured in the magazine *Le Figaro Illustré* shows Joan in full armor and her well-known short haircut.

the area on April 29 with French commander La Hire. They decided to wait for reinforcements before making any moves. But it was the first opportunity for the courage she would become known for. While French forces distracted the English on the west side of Orléans, Joan helped lead

Henry Sheffer's painting depicts Joan of Arc entering Orleans on horseback, beginning the liberation of the city from the English.

forces unopposed through the city's eastern gate. This mission included bringing in and storing important supplies.

On the evening of May 4, when Joan was resting, she suddenly jumped up, inspired, and announced that she would attack the English. Arming herself, she hurried to an English fort east of the city, where she discovered a battle already underway. Her arrival roused the French, and they took the fort.

The morning of May 6, Joan advanced on another fort. The English evacuated to defend a stronger position nearby, but Joan and La Hire attacked and took it by storm. Very early the next day, the French moved against the fort of Les Tourelles. She impressed everyone by helping lead the charge in battle several times. Joan was injured by an

JOAN OF ARC: WARRIOR WOMAN

Historians are mostly unanimous that Joan never personally killed or even injured anyone. But she certainly put herself in harm's way, including leading charges, and thus inspired those around her, and suffered for it. Squires and bodyguards guaranteed her basic safety in the heat of battle. She served more as an inspirational figure, accompanying her forces waving her banner. Being part of or even nearby any medieval battle was always risky. Behind the scenes, Joan created battle plans and managed troop movements, and crafted strategies to aggressively negotiate terms with the English when necessary.

A nineteenth-century print shows Joan of Arc rallying the French to storm the gates of the town of Les Tourelles.

arrow, but quickly returned to the fight after dressing her wound.

The troops rallied when they saw her return to the battle, and pressed on until the English surrendered. Tales of how she had inspired the troops and frightened their enemies began to spread. On May 8, the English retreated, but, because it was a Sunday, Joan refused to allow any pursuit.

CHAPTER FOUR

HEROINE OF FRANCE

The faith that the Dauphin and his supporters had placed in Joan had not been in vain. Neither had Joan's own confidence in her mission. Within nine days of her arrival at Orléans, the French broke the English siege of the city. The morale, or fighting spirit, of the troops, and of the French people at large, increased tremendously. Joan had earned the name many would use for her: the Maid of Orléans.

Joan returned to meet Charles at Tours on May 9. She wanted the French forces to continue their momentum, insisting that

In this illustration, Joan of Arc kneels before the Dauphin, who would claim the French throne largely because of her efforts.

31

they put all their efforts into taking Reims. Charles could finally be officially crowned king.

Charles hesitated, however. His advisers thought he should try to reconquer Normandy. But Joan remained stubborn. Before Reims, however, they decided to clear the English out of the other towns along the Loire River, which divided the Royal French from the English-Burgundian territories.

THE LOIRE CAMPAIGN UNFOLDS

The first stop on Joan's road to Reims was a town called Jargeau in the Loire River Valley. On June 11, Joan began a siege of the town against its 700 English defenders. After the first night, Joan demanded they surrender or be shown no mercy, but the English refused. The French responded with cannon bombardment, and eventually were able to scale the walls. Many of the defenders died. News of the high death tolls inflicted upon the English began to spread, along with Joan's growing reputation for victories.

Soon after, Joan turned their attention to the town of Meung-sur-Loire to regain an important bridge. After capturing the bridge and establishing a garrison there, they skipped both the town and castle of Meung-sur-Loire. Instead, they set their sights on Beaugency, just 5 miles (8 kilometers) away.

Beaugency's main military target was the stronghold in its center. The English abandoned the main part of town and tried to hold out in the castle as the French rained artil-

This image showing the storming of Jargeau by the French is part of a manuscript from the 1490s called *Vigiles of Charles VII.*

lery fire on them. The English eventually negotiated their exit and release with Joan and Jean II d'Alençon, a duke loyal to Charles who had become one of Joan's most dedicated friends.

One of Joan's greatest challenges lay ahead, however. When the English command learned of the French victory at Orléans, they sent an army from Paris. They hoped to win with their usual tactic of using longbows. The two armies prepared to clash near Patay, north of Orléans. But French scouts located the bowmen before they could be useful. Led by Joan's close friend, La Hire (he had begun

A STRING OF VICTORIES

Joan's military accomplishments were impressive. At Orléans, she rallied the French to effective strikes that soon forced the English to lift their long siege of the city. Victory followed victory in rapid succession, until finally Joan led the Dauphin through a hostile country to be crowned at Reims as King Charles VII.

Cannons—shown here during the siege of Orléans—had come into use during the first decades of the Hundred Years' War. They soon became a permanent part of European warfare.

Many historians have commented on Joan's instinctive military genius and her extraordinary ability to quickly master various aspects of warfare, including the use of cannons. At Orléans and in other battles, Joan distinguished herself with her abilities at strategically placing cannons—at that time, a relatively new form of warfare. In fact, Alençon, one of the senior French commanders, later testified that "everyone was astonished that [Joan] acted with such prudence and clear-sightedness in military matters, as cleverly as some great captain with twenty or thirty years' experience; and especially in the placing of artillery, for in that she acquitted herself magnificently."

praying before battle because of Joan), French cavalry cut down many bowmen, and the English horsemen retreated. The Battle of Patay was the last one in what became known as the Loire Campaign. With this great victory, Joan and her fellow commanders showed that the English were not invincible.

CROWNING THE KING

Their latest triumph made Joan believe it was time to strike while the iron was hot, so to speak. Rejoining the Dauphin nearby, she tried to convince him to attempt to take Reims and crown himself king, but he was again indecisive, and some of his advisers were, too. Joan spent a long time trying to make him see the wisdom of this decision. Finally, he decided she was right.

Joan stands behind Charles VII as he is crowned at Reims, as shown in this nineteenth-century painting by Jules Eugène Lenepveu.

Customary letters were sent out declaring Charles's coronation, and Joan and the Dauphin set out on the march to Reims on June 29. By July 16, after winning over several towns along the way, the royal army reached Reims, which opened its gates. It was also a show of force, because they had crossed territory under mostly enemy control.

On July 17, the moment she had sworn to fight for was now a reality: Charles VII was consecrated in the cathedral at Reims as ruler of France. While it changed little in the struggle between the French and the English and Burgundians, it was a huge symbolic victory. Joan was present, standing with her banner not far from the altar. After the ceremony, she knelt before Charles, calling him her king for the first time.

CHAPTER FIVE

PRISONER, MARTYR, AND SAINT

I f it were up to Joan, the French would have attacked Paris immediately. But the new monarch's hesitation and indecision prevented Joan's soldiers from a full attack. Nevertheless, Compiègne and other towns north of Paris were taken.

The closest Joan came to taking Paris was on September 8, when she and Alençon led forces against Paris's gates. This attack was driven back and Joan was again wounded. She wanted to try again, but Charles's council ordered a retreat. Charles soon disbanded his army for the winter and retired southward. Joan grew frustrated at the royal delay. Even when she was able to convince Charles and his council to allow her to fight, victories were limited.

CAPTURED

Joan rushed to Compiègne, near Paris, in May 1430 to help break a siege by the Burgundians. She fought valiantly, but English reinforcements forced their retreat. She was among the last to cross a bridge, ensuring others crossed first, when she was thrown off her horse—many claim, by an English archer. She was unable to get back on as enemies closed in. France's most inspiring and successful military leader of the war was captured.

Joan was imprisoned in a castle. She tried to escape and return to Compiègne. Her captor, John of Luxembourg, a French ally of the English and Burgundians, sent her even farther away. Her desire to escape was so great that she jumped from the top of a tower, falling into the moat. She was unconscious but not seriously hurt.

The keep, now called the Tower of Joan of Arc, is all that remains of the castle of Rouen, one of the sites where she was held during her trial and imprisonment.

Once recovered, she was taken to Arras, a town loyal to the duke of Burgundy. Under English pressure, John sold Joan to the English for a small fortune. Shockingly, Charles, who was working with the duke of Burgundy on a truce, did not try to save her.

ON TRIAL FOR HERESY

The English wanted Joan dead, but they hoped to have her tried by a religious court. The Burgundian-controlled University of Paris provided the charges of heresy and witchcraft, and provided some of the members of the court. The chief of the court was the bishop of Beauvais, Pierre Cauchon.

Joan was handed over to Bishop Cauchon on January 3, 1431. Joan appealed to be judged by the pope, and was denied. For months, she was chained, threatened with torture, and harassed with thousands of questions. Still, she had maintained her innocence, confounding the court with simple answers to tricky questions. St. Catherine and St. Margaret, she said, still counseled her. On May 23, she was condemned to be burned unless she recanted.

Faced with certain death, Joan recanted, but many historians think she did not fully understand the statement of recantation. Consequently, her punishment was commuted from death to life imprisonment. This leniency enraged the English, however, and it was not long before she was accused of relapsing from her submission.

On May 30, 1431, Joan, only nineteen years old, was turned over to the English civil authorities and burned to death at the stake in a marketplace at Rouen, France.

The Maid paid the ultimate price for her beliefs and defiance when she was burned at the stake for heresy, an unfortunately all-too-common occurrence at the time.

THE MAID ON TRIAL

Bishop Cauchon tried everything he could to trick and trip up Joan to convict her of heresy and other crimes. There were seventy charges against her, one of which was that she wore men's clothing. They were eventually dropped to twelve.

One of Cauchon's tactics was to try to force her to admit that she had made up the divine voices that spoke to her. Another charge, and perhaps the most serious, was that she preferred what she believed to be direct commands from God to the commands of the church. She held fast, saying that she was loyal to God and her saints and held herself answerable to them for her words and actions.

Threatened with torture, Joan said that even if she changed her story that she would later maintain that any statement extorted from her by force was false. Joan showed much sophistication, intelligence, and moral courage in dealing with the bishop's attempts to get her to admit to her supposed crimes.

THE LEGACY OF THE MAID OF ORLÉANS

About twenty-five years after Joan's execution, King Charles, who had settled the Hundred Years' War finally in France's favor, aided Joan's family to appeal her case to the pope and officially clear her name. In 1456, a papal court annulled the judgment of 1431.

Had she returned in the modern era, Joan probably would have been amazed to discover that she had joined the company of the very saints she had credited for her mission. She was canonized (declared a saint) by Pope Benedict XV in 1920 at St. Peter's Basilica in Vatican City, the papal enclave in Rome, Italy.

In the decades and centuries following her death, Joan's status and legend as a martyr, someone who had sacrificed her life for her cause, religion, and nation, only grew. She became not only a symbol of France that helped unite the nation, but also a role model for girls and women who rose above their social limitations in many different eras.

Before her death, Charles VII issued this letter declaring Joan's family nobility, as a reward for her loyalty and service.

In addition to paintings, books, and movies of her life and accomplishments, there are sculptures and statues of Joan of Arc all over the world. Some of the most famous exist in the French towns and cities she fought over,

This monument of Joan in Orléans is one of many that exist in France and worldwide. She remains a powerful symbol for the French, for women, and for people of faith.

including Orléans, Reims, Compiègne, and Paris. Others—in Portland, Oregon, New York City, Philadelphia, Montreal, Quebec, and New Orleans—remind visitors of her courage, steadfastness, intelligence, honesty, and strength. Many churches are named after her. For the French people and Roman Catholics, for women worldwide inspired by her example, and for anyone who admires heroism, Joan of Arc's legend lives on.

GLOSSARY

campaign A connected series of military operations forming a distinct phase of a war.

cavalry Mounted soldiers, especially knights, that made up one of the most important and feared parts of any medieval army.

chastity Abstaining from sexual activity, often for religious reasons.

chivalry The spirit or customs identified with medieval knighthood, especially honor, generosity, and courtesy.

combatant A person or other party (such as a nation) that engages in combat or war.

coronation The act or occasion of crowning a monarch.

courtier A person in attendance at a royal court.

Dauphin The term for the male heir apparent (usually the oldest son of the previous ruler) to the throne of France.

devout Devoted to a religion or to religious duties or exercises.

duchy The territory controlled by a duke or duchess.

garrison A military post, especially a permanent one.

heretic One who dissents from an accepted religious belief or doctrine.

morale The mental or emotional condition of a group of people in approaching a task, especially that of troops facing battle or war.

recant To take back publicly an opinion or belief.

royalists In the context of the Hundred Years' War, the French royalists were those loyal to the kings of France and opposed to the English and Burgundians.

siege A military blockade of a city or fortified place to compel it to surrender.

Brooks, Polly Schoyer. *Beyond the Myth: The Story of Joan of Arc*. Boston, MA: Houghton Mifflin Harcourt, 1999.

Castor, Helen. *Joan of Arc: A History*. New York, NY: Harper Perennial, 2016.

Goldstone, Nancy. *The Maid and the Queen: The Secret History of Joan of Arc*. New York, NY: Penguin Books, 2013.

Harrison, Kathryn. *Joan of Arc: A Life Transfigured*. New York, NY: Anchor Books, 2015.

Kudlinski, Kathleen. *Joan of Arc* (DK Biography). London, UK: Dorling Kindersley, 2008.

McCann, Michelle Roehm, and Amelie Welden. *Girls Who Rocked the World: Heroines from Joan of Arc to Mother Teresa.* New York, NY: Aladdin, 2012.

Pollack, Pam, Meg Belviso, and Andrew Thomson. *Who Was Joan of Arc?* (Who Was...?). New York, NY: Grosset & Dunlap, 2016.

Spoto, Donald. *Joan: The Mysterious Life of the Heretic Who Became a Saint*. San Francisco, CA: HarperSanFrancisco, 2007.

WEBSITES

Because of the changing nature of internet links, Rosen Publishing has developed an online list of websites related to the subject of this book. This site is updated regularly. Please use this link to access this list:

http://www.rosenlinks.com/WWCH/joanofarc

INDEX